Poems of Derbyshire

by Ruby Lee

DALESMAN BOOKS

1979

£1

**THE DALESMAN PUBLISHING COMPANY LTD.,
CLAPHAM (via Lancaster), NORTH YORKSHIRE**

First published 1979

ISBN: 0 85206 492 6

Printed in Great Britain by
GEORGE TODD & SON
Marlborough Street, Whitehaven

CONTENTS

Line drawings by Ruby Lee and James R. Lee.

The cover drawing is of St. Mary's church, Sutton Scarsdale.

Derbyshire

Derbyshire, my Derbyshire, amongst your hills,
Your banks, your meadows and your rocky ways
I've wandered o'er the years, and I've been happy
To know you well. How you've enriched my days!

Fine are your rivers, streams and waterfalls,
These I have loved, and these I cherish still;
Your Stately Homes, your works of art, your treasures
Are mine to see and savour at my will.

Fast fly the years, but still your beauty lingers
In every tree in Autumn, wood in Spring;
Wild flowers there are many, pleasures bounteous
In the hedgerows where the songbirds sing.

Deep in your soil there lies hope of the future,
In minerals abundant in the earth,
In crops that flourish, yielding fruitful harvests;
And all this from the county of my birth.

Loud is my praise, that in a world of turmoil,
Here lies a peace, the peace we so desire,
Amidst the hills, the rocky banks and meadows,
And streams of my beloved Derbyshire.

The Small Well at Barlow

Leaf upon leaf, petal upon petal,
Busy hands are working in the clay,
Blending all the colours of the flowers,
Pressing, hour by hour, day by day.

Many years of learning and devotion
Are embedded in each curve, each line;
Skill that's handed down through generations
Shows in patterns intricate and fine.

Prying eyes will never see the dressing,
Secrecy surrounds it to this day;
Nor can other Wells outshine the beauty
Seen as all the covers come away.

"God Save The Queen", pictures clear and simple,
Bible scenes we know only too well;
So the magic comes again to Barlow,
As we gather round the smallest Well.

Eyam

I have been to Eyam,
There is a haunted look
In every tiny cottage
And every little nook.

Time has not erased yet
From her, the tragedy
Steeped within each old wall
And every ancient tree.

I saw it in the faces
Of people, I could tell
Someone's hand had guided
The hands that dressed the well.

Villagers try to forget,
The sufferers are gone
But the memory of the plague
Ever will live on.

Derwent Water

Derwent water, flowing swiftly,
Of your sight I'll never tire
'Twixt the trees and grassy hillocks,
On and on through Derbyshire.

Twisting, turning, never stopping,
Far away at times, then near;
Sloping meadows all around you
But your melody I hear.

Beeches spread low branches o'er you,
Still I hear your friendly call
Whether you be reservoir
Or many a lovely waterfall.

May you flow along for ever,
Of your music I'll not tire,
Singing softly as you travel
On and on through Derbyshire.

The Beauty of the Dales

Nothing can surpass the beauty
Of a misty, early dawn
Breaking over Derbyshire
To reveal the dales at morn.

Lovely Ashford-in-the-Water,
Where the gently-flowing Wye
Makes her way from Monsal Dale
Where the grey cliffs loom on high.

Dovedale beckons me in sunlight.
Lathkill Dale is fresh from sleep,
All aglow with sparkling waters,
Silent valleys, hills of sheep.

Let me wander in the morning,
Stand and rest at Arbor Low
By the ancient ring of limestones,
Relics of the long-ago.

These our ancestors bequeathed us,
Quiet reminders of the past.
Roman road and tumulus,
These things were all meant to last.

Gritstone, limestone, cave and cavern,
Peak and Speedwell, Blue John, Treak,
Stalagmites and stalactites,
All the jewels of the Peak.

This land holds a wealth of treasure,
Much is still beneath our feet;
Let us come and know the pleasures
Where the hills and valleys meet.

Though my feet are ever wandering
Over hills and over vales,
Nothing can, for me, surpass
The timeless beauty of the dales.

Just a Gate

Here I stand and meditate,
Leaning on the old yard gate.
Just a gate, or so it seems,
Made of wood and nails and dreams.

Climbed by many a girl and boy,
Opening to many a joy;
Leading to familiar ways,
This gate has seen happy days.

Firm it stands, and made to last,
Through it many feet have passed,
Father, mother, daughter, son,
Workers when the day was done.

Preacher, doctor, midwife, tramp,
Guided by the old yard lamp.
People in their Sunday-best.
Some have gone through to their rest.

Creaking now, but still it stands,
Held up by so many hands.
Just a gate, or so it seems,
But this one shares all my dreams.

Hardwick Hall

Hardwick Hall invited me
To enjoy her many charms.
Cedars standing by the gateway
Welcomed me with open arms.

First of all, her tapestries
Caught my ever-searching eye,
All the years of loving toil
Were there on view to passers-by.

Furniture told such a story;
Staircases were cold and clean.
I could swear I felt the presence
Of a duchess or a queen.

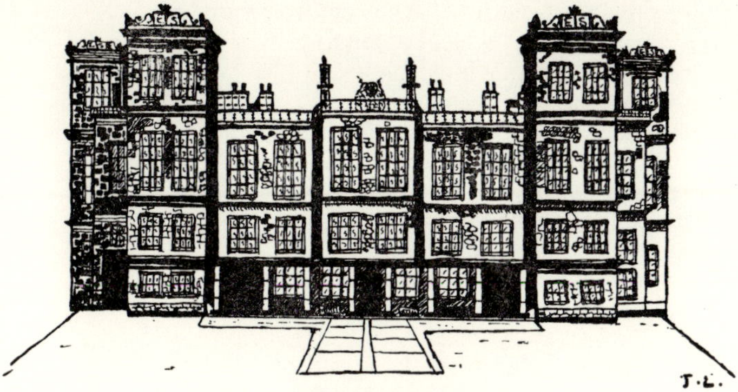

Hardwick Hall

Yes, the atmosphere has lingered
In the kitchen, on the stair,
In the portrait gallery
As generations mingle there.

Oh, the intrigue of the Chambers
And the old four-poster bed;
Mary, Queen of Scots once slept there.
There were others, long since dead.

Fragments of embroidery,
Carpets brought back from the East
All combined to give a picture
Of the splendid days of feast.

In the garden there was mystery,
Who walked here and who sat there?
In the chapel there was silence;
Did they all meet here in prayer?

I shall go again to Hardwick,
There is so much still to see.
When I do, Old Bess of Hardwick,
Will your cedars welcome me?

A Breath of Country Air

Give me a breath of the country air
And a walk in a leafy lane,
Where the soft winds blow
And the catkins grow,
And lilac hangs low in the rain.

Give me a house by a lazy stream,
With roses that bloom by the door;
Where the days are long,
And the blackbird's song
Will cheer me for evermore.

Give me a church with a steeple tall,
And a faith that will help me along;
With blue skies above
And a Christian love,
I will smile when the road is long.

Give me a heart that is happy and gay,
And a life that is free from care,
A contented home
When I cease to roam,
And a breath of the country air.

Spring Morning in Sutton Scarsdale

Glistening dewfall covers all the land,
The wakening sun comes creeping down the lane
Touching each gatepost with her dancing beams.
The silver birch is sparkling once again.

Cobwebs hang dew-heavy on the hedge
Whilst chattering sparrows tell me they're awake.
And old elm is as silent as the grave,
Though distant geese their noisy warnings make.

New lambs on the sheltering hillside bleat,
But mother ewe is ready with the milk;
And now the gorse is golden once again.
The quiet lake shines with a sheen of silk.

Grey scudding clouds of night have long since fled.
This, then, is the new and promised day.
The rooks are risen and the lark is out
As morning comes to melt the moon away.

The Hills of Home

The hills of home are far away,
Where still the purple heather spreads
Its carpet bold o'er many a mile,
And birches shake their lovely heads.

Where pheasant flaunts his brazen coat
And pewits nest in tufts of grass,
Old wily fox still runs in fear
Of hunting days that never pass.

The woodland stream meanders down
To kiss the bracken's tight-curled fronds,
Where speckled trout hide 'neath the stones
And dart away from eager hands.

Hark! New-born lambs proclaim their birth.
The barren fields are sprouting grain,
Promising a harvest, though
The old mill-wheel won't turn again.

The hills of home are far away
But still the heather calls to me.
If home is where the heart is, then
That surely is where I should be.

Bank Green Farm (Cordwell Valley)

Fox Lane always holds for me
Memories of younger days,
Ghosts of my forefathers lurk
Somewhere in its grassy ways.
And in furrows on the hills
Where the teams of horses trod,
In the garden of Bank Green,
Underneath each earthen sod.

Time has claimed the old stone house.
Weeds have sometime claimed the land.
All that's left are piles of stone,
But there's room enough to stand
Looking o'er the countryside,
Miles and miles away and more,
Where my own forefathers stood
Often, in the days of yore.

Country Lanes

Go along the country lanes
To Cordwell Valley in the Spring,
Wander by the winding brook
And listen to the blackbird sing.

Roam the lovely Smeekley woods
And up the hill to Owler Bar.
Grassy banks will welcome you
Where the rhododendrons are.

Go to where the bilberries
Provide the smoke-blue fruit for all.
Past the dainty silver birches,
On to where the curlews call.

Here you'll find a different scene
As you stand and look around,
Heather, lovely springy heather,
Finest views that can be found.

Waterfalls that come from no-where,
Vanishing into some stream.
Banks of moss and palest harebell
Invite you to sit and dream.

Climb the rocks that look o'er Baslow
Where the sheep can freely roam,
Oh, if I were but a gipsy,
This is where I'd make my home.

Roam the country lanes, my friend,
To Cordwell Valley in the Spring,
Wander by the babbling brook,
Along with it your heart will sing.

Cedars of Lebanon

Some people think the oak tree
Is the proudest tree of all,
But in my little village
We have trees both great and small.

The willow in the churchyard
Is a lovely sight to see.
There's sycamore and ash and elm
And many a chestnut tree.

The copper beech are beautiful
In mellow Autumn time,
And poplars tower above the heads
Of silver birch and lime.

The holly is a favourite
When snow is on the ground.
The cherry tree is hard to beat
When Springtime comes around.

The best trees came from Lebanon
A long, long time ago
And now they stand in majesty,
The finest trees I know.

They're old and wise and wonderful,
And there I long to be,
Beneath the lovely cedars dark,
That reach out arms for me.

A Woodland Glade

I love to walk in a woodland glade
Where the cowslips lie in the leafy shade.
Where violets abound, anemones too,
And bluebells shimmer like a sea of blue.

The beech trees sigh and cuckoos call
And join in the music of a waterfall
As it meets the brook that hurries along,
And has no time for the wild birds' song.

Let me cup my hands and drink the wine
That flows by the fern and gold celandine,
And cherish the gifts that God has made,
So that I may walk in a woodland glade.

The Crooked Spire

Derbyshire has lovely views,
Some steeped in history,
And many famous monuments
For everyone to see.
But in the heart of Chesterfield
There's a building to inspire
Great interest in all of us —
The famous Crooked Spire.

I hear the peal of your ten bells
St. Mary and All Saints.
They ring out clear for miles around
But I have no complaints.
I go and sit inside the church
Its history to acquire
And enjoy the pleasant atmosphere
Of the famous Crooked Spire.

"How did it twist?" the people ask,
This answer is but one,
The timber of the spire was warped
By warm rays of the sun.
Seven centuries or more it's stood,
'Twas almost lost by fire,
But still it points up to the sky,
The famous Crooked Spire.

But now, the face of Chesterfield
Is changing very fast
And soon there'll be few buildings
To remind us of the past.
So when I journey to the town
I linger to admire
This church with its rare feature,
The famous Crooked Spire.

Very soon we shall not have
The open market stall,
And they're wanting to demolish
The historic Market Hall.
So if you want an outing,
And if you so desire,
Then come and visit Chesterfield
And its famous Crooked Spire.

We know that progress must take place,
Old buildings will decay,
But we need something of interest
In this ultra-modern day.
And so, of many lovely views,
There's one I'll never tire
And that's the pride of Chesterfield —
The famous Crooked Spire.

The Crooked Spire

Dream of a Cottage Garden

Here I shall make a lily pond,
Encircle it with flag and frond,
And wild white daisies shall abound,
Well-sprinkled on the lawns around.

And herbs and mignonette just there
With lavender, to scent the air;
And roses, lovely roses gay,
To cheer me on a summer's day.

I'll plant a bush of golden broom,
And lilac, (if I have the room)
A shrub of orange-blossom white,
It's perfume rare for my delight.

In autumn, marigolds' bright show
Shall give me joy where'er I go.
And in the winter, snowdrops small;
And in the springtime, tulips tall.

Just here I'll rest my garden seat
On silken moss, to soothe my feet.
The silver birch shall give me shade,
(If I'm not busy with the spade).

And if, to you, it's more or less
A patch of barren wilderness,
To me a paradise it seems,
Seen only in my wildest dreams.

The Vagabond

A vagabond came passing by,
A stranger from the town;
His only friend was the soft wind's sigh,
And his only shelter, the lonely sky.

Night shall disguise his careworn face;
Cool springs his wine shall be;
An outcast of the human race,
And all he asks is a resting place.

Soft mosses shall his pillow be,
Bracken, his eiderdown.
The stars and moon his company,
For a roving vagabond is he.

Wild Violets

On my knees I search for sweet wild violets,
Moss and ferns abundant at my feet;
Beeches trail low branches in the breezes,
Where the brook and weeping willows meet.

Laying down my burdens for a moment,
Here I find tranquillity and peace
'Midst the soft and dewy gifts around me —
Nature has provided all of these.

Quiet is the woodland now, at evening;
Birds are hushed, the sun has gone to rest.
Creatures are all safely in God's keeping;
These, the precious moments I love best.

Such is the enchantment of wild violets,
Giving out their perfume through the hours,
That, in gratitude, I pray a moment,
On my knees amidst these tiny flowers.

Peace upon the Land

Grey clouds of night, borne on a summer breeze,
As dying day holds evening to her breast,
And tired creatures rustle through the trees,
These are the moments that I love the best.

Soft whispers in the gently-swaying grass,
Bees flying silently by field and gate,
And late birds homing, calling as they pass —
This is the time for me to stand and wait.

Soon, tired sheep will lie upon some hill,
Waiting until morning's gentle hand
Bids every bird and beast obey her will;
Till then, let peace descend upon the land.

Bolsover Castle

Silently she stands, serene and still,
Upon the very topmost of the hill.
Her strong walls bear the force of many a gale,
Her eyes look out far over hill and vale.

A castle old and tired, but full of pride,
What are the secrets she is trying to hide?
What could she tell me, if she had her say,
Of crimes and treason of a bygone day?

Of kings and dukes, of lords and ladies fair
Who all were entertained in splendour there?
Of fortress strong that harboured men of war,
And of the bloody battle of Marston Moor?

Old castle on the hill, aloof and stark,
Do ghosts walk in your shadows after dark
And do they, in their searching, hope to find
Some peace that long ago they left behind?

As night falls she puts on a different air
As lights go on around her, everywhere;
It's then she comes to life, as through the trees
I catch a glimpse of her dark mysteries.

How sinister she looks! How eerie now
As owl starts hooting from a nearby bough
And old man moon his nightly vigil keeps
On castles grim and everything that sleeps.

I see her next in sunlight, ghosts are gone
But all her mysteries still linger on.
Bolsover Castle, lady on the hill,
How silently you stand, serene and still.

In Meadows

The daisies are a million shining stars
Strewn at my feet, the buttercups of gold
A million blobs of sun dropped from the sky,
And all these pleasures are mine to behold.

The harebell dancing in a Summer breeze,
The humble clover that attracts the bee,
And drifts of blood-red poppies newly-born;
All these flowers bring great joy to me.

I sit here in the meadows all alone
With Nature, and for just a little while
Forget the world exists and all its gloom,
Until the sunlight creeps beyond the stile —

And purple night her curtain spreads around
All things that dwell in meadows and in trees;
Then rising from the grass I wander home
In solitude, and with a quiet peace.

Sutton Hall

Old Sutton Hall stands grim and gaunt
Against the grey of morning sky.
She's silent now, but what a host
Of memories of days gone by.

Of ladies living graciously,
And deer that roamed her lovely parks;
The carefree days of carriages,
Of lakes and shady tree-lined walks.

Now, birds have found a sanctuary,
The ghostly lady walks in peace.
Around the ruins of the Hall
She softly glides amongst the trees.

The old church bell still summons all,
As in the days of old, to pray,
So linking present to the past
If only for the Sabbath day.

Oh, monument that gazes East
To catch the sunlight and the rain,
Old Sutton Hall, long may you stand
And one day come to life again.

Nature at Her Best

I wandered down a Derbyshire lane
Where, after a shower of April rain
A cuckoo called from the bluebell wood,
And life had never felt so good.

I paused a moment and I thought
Of all the pleasures the day had brought.
Of beech trees swaying in the breeze
And violets hiding 'neath the trees.

Of moss and fern and drops of dew,
And ivy leaves all shiny and new.
Of birds just lately flown the nest,
And nature at her very best.

If only people would stop and look
At the flowers, trees and meandering brook,
Then, in this setting they would find,
Like me, a calm and a peace of mind.

Carpenter's Millthorpe

Where the lonely mill-race ran
'Neath a canopy of trees
Stood a little wooden hut,
Open to the playful breeze.

In this hut and all alone
In a shady, ferny nook
Carpenter sat, pen in hand,
Busy writing in his book.

As the mill-wheel turned nearby,
Many thoughts would fill his mind
As he sat in meditation,
Thoughts that he has left behind.

I have walked beside his brook,
Felt the coolness 'neath my feet,
Stepped into its shallow pools
Where the ferns and fishes meet.

Edward Carpenter's Hut

Felt the stones and heard the splash,
Seen the spoted trout in play,
Leaping up to catch the flies
Swarming on a Summer day.

But I've seen the village change
Over twenty years or so,
Cottages turned into mansions,
People come and people go.

Gone now is the thatched-roof shed
Where ramblers would congregate.
Royal Oak remains the same
Though Mary takes the place of Kate.

Carpenter's hut is no more,
Wheel and mill-race now are gone.
Only the meandering brook
That inspired great men, goes on.

Evening in a Derbyshire Village

Birds are winging home; soon night will fall,
A solitary thrush calls his last call.
The sky is streaked with red, bees homeward wend
And evening now approaches as a friend.

A stillness has enveloped me, the day
That gave me pleasure hurries fast away
As night sounds take the place of daytime's hum,
And stars appear, to tell me evening's come.

The promise of a fine to-morrow shows
As high up in the trees, the restless crows
Now at their roosting, rock themselves to sleep.
Bright be your light, moon, as your watch you keep.

Evening has descended o'er the fold,
Sleep O lambs, sleep on the sheltered wold.
Morning is not so very far away,
But evening has come to close a perfect day.

Limestone Walls

The limestone walls of Derbyshire
Were built by many a hand,
Making fields a patchwork quilt
Thrown across the land.

Spreading over miles of peakland,
Clean and fresh and gay,
Up the hills and down the dales,
Wandering far away.

Here, the moss has spread her mantle
O'er a silvery head.
There, within a rocky circle,
Lambs have made a bed.

At night they have a beauty rare,
Grey walls that never sleep,
Standing there like sentinals,
Guardians of the sheep.

Fashioned by our forefathers
In the days of yore,
The limestone walls of Derbyshire
Will stand for evermore.

Old Man at Crich Stand

There he stood with cap in hand,
Head bowed and in silent prayer
For his comrades lying there,
Fallen in a foreign land.

No emotion showed that day,
But I knew he felt the loss.
As he knelt and placed a cross,
All his thoughts were far away.

Sherwood Foresters of old,
Few remain to tell the story
Of the days of death and glory,
And of men so brave and bold.

Crich Stand

On the Edge of Beeley Moor

I can hear the whisperings in the heather,
In the tussocks on the Beeley moor,
Hear the soughing in the silver birches
And, though I have heard it all before —

Still it lures me, Summer after Summer
Here I sit, warm fingers touch the peat;
Dust and dirt don't bother me, I'm happy
As long as there is heather round my feet.

Whortleberries grow in great profusion
Here, where they have spread o'er many a mile;
Over yonder where a spring has surfaced,
Ramblers often linger for a while.

Here is heaven for a nature-lover
Whether he is rich or he is poor,
He can seek and find the peace he craves for
Somewhere in the heather, on the moor.

To a Rose in My Garden

O, lovely rose, your beauty's only lent
For such a brief time, but a time well spent.
I look upon you now as morning dew
Has shed her soft tears for the love of you.

I pluck you not, for it would be a crime
If you should wither, long before your time,
And so I visit you from day to day
Until one evening you just fade away.

I mourn your passing, only time will show
If in your place another rose will grow,
But even if your life was only lent
For just a brief time, 'twas a time well spent.

Return to Holmesfield

When my feet took me to Holmesfield
To re-live my childhood days,
Thoughts came to me of the thrills
Of Oadley's fair and Timmy Ray's.

I could almost hear the organ,
Melodies of yesterday
On the night breeze, through the meadows,
O'er the hills and far away.

Holmesfield has its share of history
If one only cares to look,
Old cruck barns and ancient buildings,
Mentioned in the Domesday Book.

Passing by the old school gateway,
Thoughts in conflict filled my mind
Of the days of many hardships
And of headmistress so kind.

She, our characters had moulded,
Taught us manners and the rest.
Love and care were part of schooling,
Weren't those days the very best?

As I wandered in the churchyard
Poignant feelings came to me,
Especially where my ancestors
Were buried 'neath the old yew tree.

As I looked round, there were others,
Some of old and some of late.
Deep emotions stirred within me
As I shut the old church gate.

Here I said goodbye to Holmesfield
Where once stood a castle bold.
I shall ever hold her dearly
And return until I'm old.

Old Pit Pony

I've come to see you, old pit pony,
In your clean and fresh abode;
Someone cared enough to save you;
Someone took your heavy load.

But inside your murky prison,
'Midst the dust and damp and clay,
Did you dream of fresh green pastures
Like the ones you know to-day?

You can't see me, old pit pony,
Years of darkness took their toll;
It's too late to save your eyesight,
But someone has saved your soul.

Riber Castle

Towering over Matlock
The Riber Castle stands,
Commanding views for miles around,
The finest in the land.

It may not be a castle
That harboured soldiers bold,
Nor brings to mind great battles
That raged in days of old.

But still there is a mystery
Within it's fortress walls,
And a little of the dignity
Of great and stately Halls.

The park holds varied wild-life
For young and old to view,
So if you pay a visit
There's much to see and do.

The beauty of this landmark
Is scenery it shows
Far down into the valley
Where the Derwent flows.

Riber Castle

So look to the horizon,
Many a mile away,
You'll see a dozen different views
On a fine, clear day.

So when you go to Riber,
As I'm sure you will,
May you enjoy your outing
To the castle on the hill.

Skylark

To-day I saw the skylark,
Heard her sing,
Hovering in the air
With fluttering wing;
Pure magic pouring from
Her tiny voice,
And I, with her,
Could not help but rejoice.
Sing, oh skylark,
Sing your song for me.
Tell the world below
That you are free.

Eweford Bridge

Strange, as now I stand on Eweford Bridge,
Watching busy water pass below,
That I should think of only those who built
These works of art, so many years ago.

Just a few initials carved in stone,
Left by the craftsmen of a bygone day
Is all there is to see, but often goes
Unnoticed as the people pass this way.

But in this leafy and secluded spot
Where cooling spring oft lured the passer-by,
When young, I'd play beneath this very bridge.
I knew each curve, heard every echoing sigh.

I knew each tree that generously o'er-hung
Its branches soft and green to give me shade;
And how I loved to watch the leaping trout
That in a pool swift widening rings had made.

Fat hazelnuts, that hung in clusters ripe
Just out of reach upon some slippy bank
Would tempt me, till I had to cross the brook
By way of stepping-stones that always sank.

But strangely, as I stand on Eweford Bridge,
It's not the water that I see below,
My thoughts are with the one who gave me name
And left his mark here, many years ago.

Jennie the Fox Cub

Orphaned, frightened and alone,
But rescued by some boys,
She came to know a happy life,
A life of carefree joys.

Her mistress gave her food and love,
And taught her many things,
But wondered if some day she might
Just yearn to spread her wings.

But cub so small and so content,
Was well-behaved as any,
So finally she was adopted
And was christened 'Jennie'.

All the fields and lanes she roamed,
Her mistress by her side,
And all the family and friends
Looked on with special pride.

Alas! small animals must grow,
And Jennie did the same,
But now she's gone, the woods still hear
The echo of her name.

So if in heaven foxes dwell,
Then pleasures, there'll be many
As mistress roams the lanes again,
Along with lovely Jennie.

Ode to a Wild Poppy

Envy you not the richness of a rosebud,
See how the petals open on your birth,
Crinkled, flamboyant, eagerly unfolding
As you survey this place called Mother Earth.

Although you live your life in isolation,
Still you dance gaily as the breezes blow,
So envy not the garden full of roses,
For there is room enough for you to grow.

God deemed you flourish in the self-same garden,
Gave you the same rich soil, the same soft dew,
Nurtured you in the coolness of the evening,
Folded your petals when the day was through.

And though your life is all too swiftly over,
Torn petals falling in your last repose,
You have been bold and reckless, gay and generous,
So envy not the richness of a rose.

Haytime

Have you ever sat in fields
And watched the insects as they pass,
And gathered ladies-slippers,
Chimney-sweeps and trembling grass?

Have you watched the busy bees
Collecting nectar all the day
From the clover in the meadows?
Have you smelled the new-mown hay?

Have you seen the honeysuckle
Twining in and out hedgerows,
Bryony and woody-nightshade
Climbing with the pale dog-rose?

See the foxgloves by the hedgeside,
Poppies red and speedwell blue.
Penny-moons lift up their faces,
Have you seen them smile at you?

Bee has gone home heavy laden,
Ladybird has flown away.
I must hurry ere the night comes,
Gathering in the golden hay.

Poignant Memories of Bakewell

I asked the singing river,
"Why did he have to die"?
And desolate, I gave my tears
To the passing Wye.

Bakewell on an Autumn day
Should have been for me
A pleasurable interlude,
But 'twas not to be.

Sitting by the river
In a sheltered place,
No beauty did I see that day,
I only saw his face.

They tell me Bakewell's charming
Especially in the Spring,
But no duck called to me that day,
No bird ventured to sing.

The only sounds I can recall
Were children hurrying by
And somewhere from the market-place,
A costermonger's cry.

How bittersweet the memories,
How painful the regret
Of words we left unspoken
And things undone, and yet —

I'll go again to Bakewell
When next the Spring is here,
Maybe I'll walk the riverside,
Maybe I'll shed a tear —

Perhaps I'll find the beauty
Denied to me that day,
And casting cares to the singing Wye
I'll watch them drift away.

To a Horse I Know

Horse, old tired horse in yonder meadow,
Your hunting days are o'er, but then, you know;
The grass is lush, your shelter a warm stable,
So you won't feel the icy winds that blow.

But once, I well recall, when you were younger,
Yours were the meadows, yours the heath and hill.
Over the streams and rocky banks sure-footed
You'd go, but I know you remember still.

Happy the days spent hunting with your mistress
Down country lanes, through every leafy glade,
Strong hooves a-thudding, silken mane a-flying,
Riding to hounds, oh, what a pair you made!

Long is the day now, browsing in the clover,
Dreaming of crisp dawn rides in sparkling snow.
Horse, old tired horse in yonder meadow,
Well, we're all older now, but then, you know.

A Visitor to Chatsworth

When I first set eyes on Chatsworth,
All the birds were in full song,
Trees were pushing out their buds
And lazy Derwent dreamed along.

Yellow glowed her lawns and meadows
Carpeted with daffodils;
Fallow deer roamed in her parkland,
Nestling in the lonely hills.

To this Mansion of the Peakland,
Royalty have often been,
Hers the hospitality
That welcomes commoner or Queen.

In the house, along with others
I received a welcome warm
As I viewed her many treasures
In the rooms of quiet charm.

All the history of centuries,
Years of intrigue, love and power
Concentrated in her walls
Cannot be savoured in an hour.

Fountains played amidst her gardens,
Tumbling waters of Cascade,
Emperor the wonderful
What a lovely sight these made!

Marble statues took my fancy,
These were made in Italy,
But here Paxton's name lives on
Amongst each plant and every tree.

I paused by the rhododendrons
And by the Azalea Dell,
Here I wondered if such beauty
Lasts for ever. Who can tell?

When I said goodbye to Chatsworth,
To her fountains and her deer,
Promises were made to her
That I'd return again next year.

Song of Autumn

I heard the song of Autumn,
It came upon the breeze,
Whispering in the dry hedgerows
And sighing through the trees.

It told me that the green leaves
Would soon be turned to gold,
And all the flowers of the fields
Would suddenly grow old.

I heard the sound of cornfields
Falling to the ground;
I listened for old Summer's song,
But she made no sound.

Gone was she in silence,
Taking all her mirth,
Leaving remnants of her passing,
Scattered o'er the earth.

I heard the song of Autumn
Within my heart to-day,
It stirred a host of memories
Of a yesterday.

Of ploughing and of sowing,
Of fresh and fertile field,
And how the sunshine came along
To promise a good yield.

Golden are the cornfields,
Though the grain is gone.
Garnered is my harvest now,
But gleaning follows on.

A Swan in the Park

Of all the beauteous things to look upon,
What creature could be lovelier than the swan?
I watch her glide with perfect grace and ease,
And what else could she but a poet please?

Her pure and noble form makes my heart sing;
Her tenderness for young beneath safe wing;
On clear blue waters now to me they ride,
Like some small galleon, billowing with pride.

Oh, swan, if I could only be like you,
I'd take you far away to waters new
To spend my time forever gazing on
My beautiful, enchanting, snow-white swan.

Beauty on the Waste Land

On the waste land and embankments
There is beauty to be found
In the flowers growing bravely;
Spare the time to look around.

I have seen the golden mulleins
Standing stately, just to-day.
Rose-bay willow-herb's pink spires
Have oft cheered me on my way.

Lupins blue and yellow toad-flax
Clothe the railway banks in style,
And a single hollyhock, once
Brought me pleasure for a while.

Share these momentary blessings
As you journey to and fro,
Linger as you pass the waste land
And great pleasure you will know.

Mother Nature in her wisdom
Broadcasts seed across the land,
Blown by winds to barren places
To be nurtured by God's hand.

September

September is a lovely month,
A-mushrooming I go,
With fruits of Autumn all around
And berries hanging low.

What care I if feet are wet
With early-morning dew?
It's harvest time, so come along
It's here for me and you.

Nuts and fruits and ripe berries,
Who could ask for more
Than sharing all this bounty
From Mother Nature's store?

Harvest Festival

To this little church we come so quietly
Bearing gifts of fruit and flowers gay.
Once again this is our Harvest Festival,
This, the villagers own special day.

Sheaves of corn brought by a local farmer,
Apples rosy from a little boy
Find a place in church amongst the offerings,
This, a time of giving and of joy.

Time to thank the Lord for all His goodness,
For His bounty from the generous fields.
Time to be to-gether and be grateful
For the fruits the golden harvest yields.

Flowers fill the church in every corner,
Lovingly arranged by willing hands.
Let us kneel and place our hands to-gether,
Remembering the poor of other lands.

"All is safely gathered in", we chorus,
Let the rain and stormy weather come,
This is our own service of thanksgiving,
Let us raise the song of Harvest-home.

Meditation

In the cool of the day when all is at rest,
This is the time that I love the best,
When birds are hushed and the sun long gone
And there's many a thought to ponder on.

Then I watch the moon on her weary climb
And this is my meditation time,
As the soft dew falls to cleanse the leaves,
Bestirring birds that sleep in the eaves.

Whilst trees stand vigil, the garden sleeps,
A silence descends and the willow weeps,
The daisies fold and new buds are born
Before the lark can herald the morn.

Then sorrow and joy both fill my mind
As long-forgoten paths I wind
And slumber is so very far away
When all is at rest, in the cool of the day.

Chestnut Time

Green chestnut shells,
Once candles on a tree,
Burst and spill out
Their shiny nuts for me.
Long months I waited
While the freezing rime
Clung to the trees —
They call it Wintertime.

Then Spring arrived,
This tree she chose to bless
With long white blossoms
For her bridal dress.
Warm Summer came
To swell the ripening fruit;
I often passed by,
But the tree stood mute.

The Autumn winds
Had quite a lot to say,
They shook the tree
And made her groan and sway.
I hurried out
And in the gale's short lull,
Bent low my head
And gathered pockets full.

Derbyshire Miners

Down, down they go into the bowels
Of this crusty earth
Where man is just a man, and has
To slave for all he's worth.

No pleasures to accompany them,
A moaning here and there,
A murmur of the sea, perhaps,
Coming from God-knows-where.

No bird has ever sung down there,
No air has smelled so damp,
No light has ever been as welcome
As a miner's lamp.

No. 2 Shaft, Markham Colliery

What lures them underneath the ground,
Far, far into the earth
'Midst layers of death, while up above
All nature's giving birth?

I ponder on this mystery
As I survey my coal.
What a price they've paid for this
In body, heart and soul.

Up, up they come and breathe again
The air that is divine,
And smoke the smoke that's been denied,
The tea, to them, is wine.

They do not talk of tragedies,
Of Lofthouse water's rage,
Nor of their mates at Markham
And the crashing of the cage.

For soon their bodies will uncurl,
But one of them will pack,
He's carried the weight of a million feet
Too long on his back.

Late Autumn in the Woods

When spiders spin their lacy shawls
And hang them out to dry
Upon the hedgerows in the lane,
Down to the woods go I.

The leaves are dead, the bracken too,
Forgotten berries fall like rain
And mingle with the leafmould
To nourish mother earth again.

Where beech-nuts crunch beneath my feet
And squirrel leaps from tree to tree,
Old toad sits underneath the leaves
And croaks his mournful song to me.

This is the time when life is dormant,
Trees will rest, their work is o'er.
Wild life scents the winter's start
And hurriedly finds food to store.

Mist enshrouds the wooded kingdom
But my walk is not in vain.
Nature tells me, after resting,
She will start her work again.

The Barlow Hunt

Over wild moorland, the stream and the valley,
Over the fallow, the dale and the hill,
Ride with the Barlow, horn is a-sounding,
Hounds are a-baying, all set for a kill.

Swift runs the fox, he is panting and praying,
Hoping he'll make it to yonder safe dell;
Hurry fox, hurry! Your life is as precious
As horses and hounds and the huntsman as well.

Red jackets, black jackets, women and children
Join in the sport that is favoured by kings,
Gaily they ride now, but only the fox knows
The fear and the terror a hunting day brings.

Starting at Horsleygate, over to Cartledge,
Brindwood, Highlightley, up Johnnygate Lane
To Moorhall and Fox Lane, Smeekley and Owler Bar,
Lydgate to Holmesfield and back once again.

Home is the fox, tired but safe in his dark earth.
Horn now re-echoes o'er hillside and glen.
Home go the Barlow, home to make merry
And wait till it's time to go hunting again.

The Horse-Drawn Plough

I stand at the edge of this field of grain,
Where the green ears wave and bow,
And echoing over the countless years,
Comes the sound of a horse-drawn plough.

This field has known stubble and plough and wheat
For as long as I care to recall,
And deep in it's furrows it knows of men's boots
And monotonous thud of hoof-fall.

But mechanisation has come to the land,
And we should have no cause for regret,
For the harvest can safely be gathered in now,
And the fields quickly ploughed up — and yet

I stand at the edge of this field of grain,
Where the gold ears wave and nod,
And I still hear the clink of the burnished brass,
And the sound of the shire-horses' plod.

Then my mind goes back to the golden days,
To the mill and the home-made bread,
And I see a small miracle wrought from wheat,
And a craft that will one day be dead.

But though times will change (for the better, I pray)
A nostalgia comes to me now
As I stand at the edge of this field, and hear
The sound of the horses and plough.

Across the Derbyshire Moors

Far, far away they are merging to-gether,
The soft grey of rocks and the purple of heather,
Pale blobs of sheep and the blue of the sky
And fluffy white clouds as they gather on high.
But come with me closer and soon you will see
That the sky is as blue as it ever could be.
The heather has flowers of many a hue
And even the rocks are all different, as through
Comes tumbling the cool, foaming waterfall,
Where green grow the ferns and where birches small
Give shade to the sheep, grazing all the long day
By a happy stream, that winds its way
Through grass, close cropped, where you and I
Will tarry awhile watching clouds drift by,
Till the evening comes and it merges to-gether
The grey of the rocks and the purple of heather.

The Tramp

A happy man the tramp must be,
He never wants for company.
All the animals are his friends
On his nature walk that never ends.

He knows red squirrel, badger too,
The big brown hare and the tiny shrew.
He talks to weasel and burrowing mole
And tired old dormouse in his hole.

Nuts and berries are his fare,
Of worldly troubles he has no care.
His clothes are shabby, his beard is long
But on he goes with a cheery song.

Then, when the moon is overhead,
Beneath the stars he'll make his bed,
Morning comes and he's off again
Up the meadows and down the lane.

Farmers all know him by sight,
He'll use their barns on a wintry night,
But though he has no fixed abode
He's a happy gentleman of the road.

Silver Birch

From seed tossed by careless, laughing breezes,
Life began one warm and sunny day;
She grew lovely through the changing seasons,
Making my world richer for her stay.

In the Springtime days, she wore her tassels,
Put on her own special kind of show;
Gave a rare and magical performance
In the gold of sunset's afterglow.

Summer often saw her dancing gaily
To the soft lilt of melodious breeze;
Flaunting her new flowing, silken tresses,
Trying to outshine the other trees.

Through the mellow days that came with Autumn,
Rich and gay and bountiful was she,
Tossing all her pennies to the wild winds,
Generous for all the world to see.

Then, caught up in Winter's cold embraces,
When the other trees had naught to wear,
She put on her envied silver lamé,
Sprinkled sparkling diamonds in her hair.

In the magic days that followed after,
She was chosen Queen on Winterland,
Ruling the enchanted wooded kingdom;
Silver doves kissed her bejewelled hand.

So she lived her life in gay abandon,
Pleasing all who sought to cross her path.
So she died, as mad gale swept the woodland,
Died because she could not bear his wrath.

Now she lies here, arms outstretched and broken,
Silver garments strewn amongst the grass;
Mourned by all who saw her great beginnings,
Kissed by sobbing wild doves as they pass.

But her seed lies somewhere in the woodland,
Hidden underneath the melting snow,
Waiting for the Spring to bring the warm sun,
And the carefree, laughing breeze to blow.

Across the Vale

Across the vale I stand and gaze,
Where berries black hang by the wood;
The ploughman starts his daily toil,
Morning is warm and life is good.

It seems so short a time since seed
Was sown across this fertile land,
But now the harvest, safely stored,
Has given way to Nature's hand.

No rest has she, but moving on,
She works according to a plan,
A nourishing, a sowing, then
A harvesting, all helped by man.

Then ploughing time comes round again,
A sunny day, a shower of rain.
How great the wonders of the earth,
Repeated time and time again!

These are the changing sights I see,
As often o'er the vale I gaze;
I store these golden memories,
To last me through the darkest days.

Looking at Birds

Sometimes I stand still
And look at the birds.
What could they tell me
If they had the words?

Sometimes they stand still
In fields, all alone,
Standing and waiting
As still as a stone.

What do they wait for
On long winter days?
The end of season?
The sun's warming rays?

They cannot tell me.
I never will know
Why they are waiting
Out there in the snow.

Sometimes I think,
As I look at still birds,
Thoughts that are oftentimes
Too deep for words.

The Motorway

The motorway has come to us
And changed our way of life.
It's cut right through the village
Just like a surgeon's knife,
Taking all the traffic
From the small byways.
Rushing people to the coast
For their holidays.

Humming and a-buzzing
All through the night,
Sounding horns, screeching brakes
At early-morning light.
This way and that way,
Rushing up and down.
One way goes up to the North,
The other, London Town.

But we all like progress,
So we must be fair.
It must be very useful
Or it wouldn't be there
Slicing through the village,
So we mustn't frown,
Come on, get your hat and coat,
We'll go to London Town.

The Brass Lamp

See the lamp, so old and mellow,
Glowing from the inglenook;
Mother's sewing by the fire;
Father reads his well-worn book.

This brass lamp holds many secrets;
Handed down through changing years,
It has shone for generations,
Shared their laughter and their tears.

Old horse brasses hung on leather,
Tell of days in furrows deep.
Warming-pans hung o'er the fireplace,
Tell of nights in well-earned sleep.

Jugs and bowls and copper kettles,
Burnished candlesticks and trays;
Oh, what stories to be woven
Round these treasures of old days.

Plaques of ships down through the ages,
Galleons on a stormy sea,
Toasting-forks that saw, each winter,
Gatherings round the fire for tea.

Brass and copper, old and mellow,
Gleaming from the inglenook.
Mother's dozing by the fire;
Father drops his well-worn book.

Yuletime Gathering

Curled-up brown leaves, holly berries reddening,
A nip in the air and the snowflakes flurry by.
Warm fires glowing through the friendly windowpanes.
Bright stars twinkling in the frosty sky.

Birds are sheltering in the dark, dry hedgerows,
Small voices echoing down the snowtopped hills;
Crackling yule logs in the hearth are burning bright,
Warm hands are welcoming, banishing night chills.

Families gathering in the flickering candlelight.
Old songs of Christmas sung around the tinselled tree.
Peace and goodwill, this is the unending toast,
And hope of a better world in the years to be.

Christmas comes to the Village

A still is in the air, a holy feeling
As we gather in the church to pray.
Hush now, for the children are all kneeling,
Giving thanks to God on Christmas Day.

Thanking Him for all His blessings holy,
And for all the gifts that He bestows;
Asking Him to give the poor and lowly
Food and shelter, when the chill wind blows.

In the silence of the church we listen,
Hark! The sheep are calling from the hills.
Snow is falling, soon the world will glisten,
How my heart with joy and pleasure fills!

So it must have been on Christmas morning
In Bethlehem, so many years ago,
A bright star shone, a brighter day was dawning,
Christ had come to set the world aglow.

In His honour, hear the church bells pealing,
Sending happy people on their way;
As we leave the church a peace comes stealing
Over all, this lovely Christmas Day.